JUST LISTEN

KING SPEAKS

Korrie D. Morrow

DEDICATION

I dedicate this book to my family members whose spirits have been committed into the hands of the Lord - to my father, Felipe Morrow; my grandfather, Henry Pendleton; my grandmother, Clarkye Pendleton; my great grandfather, Freeman Morrow; and my great-grandmother, Rachel Morrow. They all made this possible by raising me up to be a God-fearing man.

I also devote this book to my family members who are still here including my mother, who's always been there for me to lean on in the time of trouble. She has always given me wisdom and a better understanding of life through the Word of GOD!

To my Aunt Claudette who also gives me spiritual wisdom in the time of need. To all of my siblings including my sister Kahlea, and my two younger brothers, Kortez and Kashawn Morrow. And to all of my cousins and family members all over the world.

To my son, Korrie Morrow, Jr., for being the light to my heart and to Christina Rodgers for putting up with me.

And, last but not least, to Daisha McClain for putting up with me.

ACKNOWLEDGEMENTS

Thanks to my dad, Felipe Morrow, for teaching me to never hold back and for imparting his wisdom to me.

Thanks to my mother, Shanda Evans, for her incredible insight and wisdom and for helping me to write this book.

I also want to thank my aunt, Claudette Pendleton, for proofreading and editing my book and for imparting her insight and wisdom.

Thanks to everyone on Instagram & Facebook for their awesome support.

Table of Contents

THE TRUTH WILL MAKE YOU FREE

You are not a child. You are an adult, and but not even a child should be lied to. So, how much more – YOU!

This is a book – a weapon to assist those of you who are in a bad relationship. It will help you to WAKE UP if you allow it to!

In this book, you will receive tools to get you ready for a new and better season in your life. The book consists of simple reading, but it is filled with insight to prepare and discipline you into becoming an unpretentious, happier person while living in a shady world.

So put on your seat belt and get ready for a real ride! Just LISTEN!

Break the Cycle! Don't you know it's time to stop receiving counterfeit relationships into your life that will not enhance your future? That's right, I'm talking about those relationships that make absolutely no sense! So, break the Cycle!

Would you be concerned if you had a dog that only came home twice a week?

Then, stop entertaining that individual – your significant other that calls you, *only*, when he or she wants to have sex! He wants to feed off of your kind heart and, then, when he gets tired of you, what does he do? That's right, he moves on to the next.

TAKING A STAND

Are you really ready for a change? If you're really ready for a change, you must be willing to rid yourself of the poisons in your life – the negative people and negative surroundings in your life, that is. It is a MUST! There's no room for compromise on this one.

Walking away will show active faith instead of settling and remaining inactive. You have to be fed up with the counterfeits and lies in your life that have held you back for so long. You've got to know your own self-worth!

LISTEN! Listen to the signs that your heavenly Creator gives you. Listen to that mother's voice, that father's voice, or the heavenly voice that shouts out to you and says "THIS IS NOT RIGHT!"

UNDERSTAND AND KNOW THIS! What you allow will continue! Place your faith in God, the Creator - not in the creations. God will be to you what no man or woman could ever be!

LETTING GO OF THE PAST

Resist the temptation and pull back from seeing the significant other. Keep motivating yourself to stay focused. Stop holding down this less than a man and getting all emotional with him and acting like you are his mother.

You need a man who can hold his own and lead you.

For the right man - you are his strength, but he is your leader.

But when it's the wrong man - he puts himself in a situation that makes him look like he's your son instead of being your man.

And woman, if you have a child, please stop it. You don't need a man like that. This type of mentality, in a man, desires for a woman to take care of him because he has no insight or understanding of his own abilities, strengths, or talents. Therefore, he depends on your abilities, strengths, and talents to get him through each day. How sad is that? And, you can forget about thinking you can change him. He has to want to change himself. You cannot change anyone. You can only change yourself!

Now, on the other hand, if that's the kind of man you are looking for, then YOU MIGHT AS WELL JUST STOP HERE!

HAVING RESPECT FOR YOURSELF

Are you in a relationship that doesn't allow you to say what you want and you're being manipulated and controlled?

Are you're always thinking about the other person's needs and never your own?

If your significant other makes you feel like you are always wrong or is the cause of your low self-esteem, it is time to give yourself an evaluation on who you are and decide whether you are properly loving yourself.

First of all, you must understand that you won't be able to make good and right decisions if you are angry and emotional. You can only accomplish this when you are confident in yourself and in God.

Now if you are ready to listen, here are a few things you need to do:

Number one - stop holding on to a cheating, lying, back stabbing little boy who obviously has no idea of what it is to be a man.

Oh yeah, I am going to give you a few real instructions!

Two - stop thinking that he will change! He won't!

You Hear King?

Three - I need you to focus on yourself and your children if you have children.

Focus on obtaining a better job, making more money to take care of yourself and your children, and mostly establishing a closer relationship with God.

A true relationship with God will genuinely strengthen you and enhance your future!

If your so-called mate is making you cry, and then later he's crying in your ear talking about how he loves you and wants you back...

LET HIM CRY! (FAKE)
HE DOESN'T CARE ABOUT YOU! (TRUTH)

STAY STRONG AND KEEP MOVING FORWARD

Life goes on baby girl!
I know you are sweet and kind hearted.
You really think that this is the way you are supposed to be and that he will love you more for being a fool for him.

But it is high time for you to **queen** up! So you can meet your assigned king!

So, forget the past. This is how you will move towards your future. You won't be able to move into your future, if you're still HOLDing on to the past. See, the past HOLDs you up!

You may not be able to see the change right away but, in time, you will start to see that God has a plan for your life! However, you have to *release the past* in order to keep moving forward to see His plan!

Be patient, strong, and diligent.

No, you don't have to forget that he treated you like nothing. Remembering will keep you from going backwards. However, do forgive. Forgive him for *your* mental and emotional health. It will release you from all negativity and strife in your heart. Yes, it is time for you to truly move on with your life. You've been wallowing around this mountain too long!

NEVER BE NUMBER TWO

If your guy or girl is someone who has to always consume the attention of others, leave that person where they're at! You deserve so much more.

You are God's creation and He made you beautiful.

If you feel like you are number TWO and have expressed this concern to your significant other, yet he will not LISTEN, then guess what, it's time for you to LISTEN to these instructions.

Ask God for direction! If this someone is your assigned mate from God, God will give you the tenacity to wait on him to stop acting like a fool while you are continuing to do right by him or her.

If this is not your assigned mate from God, then YOU NEED TO STOP WASTING YOUR VALUABLE TIME!

PROTECT YOUR CHILDREN

The most precious and most valuable thing in your life should be your mind, your heart, and spirit.

See… if you can't protect the thing that gives you focus, concentration, and authority to say no when you need to, then you won't be able to protect your children, either. You need to think straight and be a strong person in order to be a blessing to your children.

Stop allowing these boys to come around your daughters and your sons!
If they will disrespect you, what do you think they will do with your children? They will disrespect your children. Count on it!

Stop allowing your daughter to walk around your man with booty shorts. This is nonsense and the Bible refers to them as silly women (2 Timothy 3:6).

Men and women, stop leaving your children any and everywhere to be taken advantage of and abused just because you want to have a good time. Just because a person appears to be okay doesn't mean that he or she is okay.

There is something called 'secret sins'. And these very people you're leaving your precious babies with, just may have them! It is time to be more responsible with the precious lives you've been entrusted with!

RECOGNIZE YOUR WORTH

ONE OF THE WORST FEELINGS IS TO FIND OUT THAT YOU WERE NOT THE ONLY ONE BECAUSE YOU DIDN'T LISTEN TO THE WARNING SIGNS AND YOU DID NOT PAY ATTENTION!

DON'T WORRY! He did not recognize the diamond that you are. He did not see that glimmer in your eyes that said, "I will be here forever."

Did you know that diamonds last forever?

Well, sometimes men get into relationships for the wrong reason. They, actually, only want a temporary fix to 'tide them over' as the saying goes, until they can get to the next woman. And, they'll tell you just about anything to get that fix. Yes, even if it means telling you, "I love you," while knowing it is not true.

YOU MUST REALIZE THAT YOU ARE A JEWEL - A DIAMOND THAT MUST BE TREATED AND HANDLED WITH SPECIAL CARE.

Now, you are no longer a baby that has to be told three or more times before you hear and understand that danger is ahead of you.

You are now a grown woman who has also grown in greater wisdom throughout your trials and troubles. And one day you will understand that the right king assigned to you will also need a treasured Proverbs 31 woman who knows what it means to be an honorable woman, worthy of respect, but, also, knows how to repay proper respect to her king.

Listen, Proverbs 31 woman, your assigned king from the Lord will love you and care for you. He will be designed for you in every way. You only need to trust in the Lord with all your heart, all your mind, and all your soul, and He will direct your paths.

WANTING SOMEONE WHO DOESN'T WANT YOU

You will miss your assigned king or queen MESSING AROUND WITH A PERSON WHO DOESN'T GIVE YOU THE PROPER ATTENTION.

SOME of you are even dating married men and women.

Wait until he is free because otherwise you are just entertaining a lie!!!

Think about it! If you have the spirit of a girlfriend, men will only entertain you as just that - a girlfriend - someone to play with. But, when you have the spirit of a wife, in due season, your assigned mate will find you!

So, wake up and get it straight! Stop settling for less and open up your heart to be willing to wait on your assigned mate whom God intended for you to spend the rest of your life with. Don't just settle for being a PLAY TOY!

WHEN THE PERSON IS NOT WORTH A DIME AND YET YOU ARE STILL INVESTING YOUR TIME, YOU ARE GIVING YOURSELF TO NO RETURN.

It is just like investing in stock that never yields a return. So, Don't Do IT!!!

Stay strong my brother or sister!

God said that He will make a way of escape for you. The key is…when the way of escape has been made – ESCAPE! Don't linger, don't ponder, and don't wonder – Just take the High Road OUT and ESCAPE!

And because you're taking the time to read this book, I KNOW YOU ARE GOING TO MAKE IT!

I wrote this book to not only encourage you but to let you know that you will be able to breathe at the end of the tunnel.

The journey you are on is to make you a stronger and better person.
You will be able to help someone else when you've mastered this test.

God will strengthen you and He will get the glory out of your life! You only need to trust in Him and He will see you through!

STEPS TO MOVE FORWARD

You will not forget this experience too quickly and it is for a reason. God wants you to ponder on it so that you will not make the same mistake twice!

Again I say, "*Forgive* those who have done you wrong so that you can move forward in life and no longer have to think on them all of the time."

If you *choose not to forgive,* you will find some way to get revenge and this will only pull you right back into the game.

Absolutely no sex, no contact, or any conversation with this person during your healing process.

No more entertaining this little boy toy. *Remember!* No more investing your time in a man not worth a dime!

It is so important to get an understanding! So, understand this! You are in fact not a side chick! You will not be treated like garbage! Let me remind you who you are.

YOU ARE A DIAMOND. This is not to say that you are better than anybody else or should walk around arrogantly, but you should know, woman, that you are worthy to be treated with respect and honor just as you give respect and honor!

Therefore, YOU MUST BE NUMBER ONE AND THE ONLY WOMAN in the relationship! You do not share a man! IF YOU'RE NOT THE ONE AND ONLY, IT'S

TIME FOR JACK TO HIT THE ROAD AND DON'T COME BACK NO MORE!

Can I go deeper and keep it real?
He REALLY just wants to get his rocks off!

I CAN TELL THAT YOU ARE HURT, BUT UNLIKE THE OTHERS I CAN GIVE YOU SOME TOOLS THAT WILL KEEP YOU FROM EVER BEING A FOOL AGAIN BABY GIRL.

I KNOW YOU HAVE HEARD THIS MAYBE A MILLION TIMES BUT JUST LISTEN OKAY.

DON'T ALLOW THAT CHEATING, LYING, SELFISH, ABUSIVE, LITTLE, BOY DOG TO MAKE YOU GIVE UP ON LIFE OR LOVE JUST BECAUSE HE HAS NO HEART OR FEELINGS.

Keep the faith and sincerely learn to trust God for your soul mate. *Think about it!*

Jesus is the one who created and instituted the marriage relationship. He's the one who created the woman for the man, so isn't it wise for us to seek Him regarding who our mates really are!

God is love! The Master of True and Real Love. *So, when it comes to getting the Real Thing and searching for a Real Love*, as the song goes - Guess what, God is the One who knows without a shadow of a doubt who is right for each and every one of us! Wait on Him!

So, keep the faith, baby girl. And know that if you trust God, He will lead you in the right path!

RULE #1: NEVER SETTLE FOR BEING #2

The BIGGEST mistake that I believe you can ever make is to not love yourself enough to *LET GO*!

But it's never too late to drop that user and abuser.

You are a gift to humanity! God made you wonderful. He says to you woman, "You are fearfully and wonderfully made" (Psalm 139:14).

I believe you can do it. I believe THAT GOD WILL GIVE YOU THE STRENGTH TO DO IT WHEN YOU ARE WEAK. You only need to trust in Him!

The Bible teaches us that God will make us strong in our weaknesses when we call on Him (Psalm 50:15). Anyone who is bent on hurting you and lowering your self-worth must go. If a person is doing nothing but taking you backwards, that person must go! He or she will only cause your mindset to be lowered. This is not a healthy relationship. Don't settle for being #2, #3, 4 or 5. RUN!

NEVER TOO LATE TO START OVER

My mother has always told me, "What is before you is greater than what is behind you."

YOUR LATTER WILL BE GREATER THAN YOUR FORMER!

WHY? BECAUSE... ALL THINGS WORK TOGETHER FOR THE GOOD TO THEM THAT LOVE THE LORD! (Romans 8:28)

When you hurt, it is a sign revealing that something is wrong. The pain is signaling you to WAKE UP! It is a Cry for you to "Do Something!"

When you go to the doctor because you feel pain, it is a sign that you need some type of treatment to heal the hurt.

Sometimes the pain requires a natural treatment and sometimes pain requires spiritual treatment and sometimes, both spiritual and natural are needed. Whatever or whichever treatment you need, just Get It! Don't wait. Get the help you need, baby girl, so that you can finally be free!

I hope that I can be an instrument to give you information and advice in your time of finding out who you are and how you really want your life to be.

KEEP YOUR RELATIONSHIP LOW KEY

KEEPING YOUR RELATIONSHIP LOW KEY IS THE BEST ADVICE I CAN GIVE YOU.

Please believe King when I tell you this!

There are people just waiting to interfere and destroy a happy home or good relationship.

There are haters including family members, fake friends, and devious individuals who just want to have sexual relations with your significant other so that they can kill your spirit.

Be careful who you vent to. You just can't trust everybody. Some of them are nothing but snakes who are just waiting to knock on your front door when you are away.

The *serpent* got to Eve while Adam was away. Think about it!

Why do you think that is? Because snakes wait for a sign of weakness and then they prey on your weakness!

This is a great pointer for you to ponder on so that you can be more relationship smart when you truly meet your king or queen!

Kings and queens don't come by the dozen. So, I'm referring to THE ASSIGNED MATE FROM ABOVE! WHEN HE OR SHE ARRIVES, GUARD WHAT IS VALUABLE!

DON'T SAY IT IF YOU DON'T MEAN IT

My ex taught me that not every person who says, "I love you" is real.

But what doesn't kill you can make you stronger dear if you allow it to.

Your ex is an ex for a reason!

That is, so you can spend your time fixing what's been broken in your life as well as taking the time needed to build yourself up, completely wake up, and officially walk away from a horrible situation.

THE IMPORTANT THING IS TO LEARN FROM EVERY ONE OF YOUR MISTAKES. THEY ARE LIFE LESSONS. THEY WILL HELP YOU TO BE EVEN MORE PREPARED FOR YOUR FUTURE TRUE MATE IF YOU CHOOSE TO LEARN FROM THEM.

Just Listen - I know it's Getting Good!

NEVER CHASE SOMEONE

When you feel anxious to see him or her, you have to stay busy doing something else. You must renew your mind by occupying your mind and thoughts with something else now!

That anxiousness is like a rush to make you call him or her or to go see the person you've become obsessed with.

Stop yourself!

Train yourself to do something else during that time until the anxiousness goes away. It will go away! You just have to put in the effort to stay free!

Again if you find yourself feeling quite lonely and in despair, find something to do that will take your mind off of that person! Spend quality time with your family or a friend that is positive and understands your situation and has no ulterior motives.

Here are a few suggestions that have worked for many in this situation...

Pray
Talk to a mentor
Read a book - read my BOOK!!!

LOVING FROM A DISTANCE

Loving from a Distance - It Just Doesn't Work!

Your mind will wander and your thoughts will imagine. So this is what I suggest baby girl.

Get your mind on things that are above him. You know, things like your education, that business that you've always dreamed about, and the importance of being treated like a queen, and, therefore, not submitting to junk.

Don't forget that you were mistreated. Remember how he left you and never called you back for days because he was with who knows who.

Focus on your NEW! This is your time for a NEW Season to manifest.

Stop holding on to how he used to treat you right.

That time is gone and God wants you to become the person He originated you to be – happy and peaceful.

LENDING YOUR GOOD HEART TO THE WRONG SOMEONE WILL GET YOU HURT

Nothing is more humiliating as being let down and embarrassed by someone you were down for.

Cheaters and liars don't change overnight okay!

They know you love them and are crazy for them. So, this makes them even more pride-filled to continue to use you even the more.

They presume that they can have sex with you whenever they want to and that they will never get you pregnant. Yet, when you do get pregnant, what do they do? They dictate to you over and over again, all through the pregnancy, that the baby may not even be their seed.

Woman, listen to me, Get your mind in order and *take a stand* even if it hurts. Yes, with this guy, there's no more need to be calling him up just to say, "Hi," instead you should be saying, "Baby Bye. It's time for this mess of a relationship to die!"

You will thank me in the end!

A LOSS IS SOMETIMES A GAIN

Never fight over someone.

If you are fighting over someone, it is clear that you are obviously not the one and only.

If your so-called significant other is entertaining other men and/or women, your attitude and decision should be that the others can just have *that mess.*

You may be feeling down but you should be very grateful that you've made up your mind not to continue investing all of your life and time with this character.

You are free now to love and focus on the betterment of yourself and your future.   Place your mind on God and He will give you *unspeakable joy.*

The Bible teaches us to seek God first (Matthew 6:33). This is why we are, oftentimes, so unhappy in life because we seek a relationship with others first and seek after things instead of establishing a relationship foremost with THE ONE WHO HAS ALL OF THE LOVE AND ALL OF THE ANSWERS ON HOW TO LOVE AN EARTHLY WOMAN OR MAN.

MEN AND WOMEN WILL FAIL YOU BUT GOD WILL NEVER FAIL YOU

In life, there is something called good or positive control, but there is also bad control. Good control guides and helps you to become better and stronger in the world just as a parent does with his or her children, for example. Bad control suppresses and destroys your life, your will, and self-esteem. God does not want us to be controlled in a bad way. This is why He created us to be free-will agents. He wants us to love and serve Him with our whole hearts and of our own free will.

Now, you can either refuse to listen or you can choose to be a person who realizes that God is the real answer to all of your questions and say to yourself, "I am going to do it His way from now on."

Stop putting your trust in man. Man is not equipped in his existence to be perfect in any way. We get so hung up on sex, looks, how much money a person makes, etc. to the point that we can't even see what really matters in a relationship. He or she is *not* God. Although, he may think he is and she may think that she is a goddess, we are created in the image of God, but we are Not God!

We are not to take advantage of people. God is pure and kind hearted and merciful. But He is also the all-wise God of judgment. So, we definitely need to take heed to how we conduct ourselves in life.

Stop allowing a man to take advantage of you by demanding that you pay a grown man's rent.

You are not a stupid woman, but you will be treated as such if you continue to act as such. Keep in mind that 2 Timothy 3:6 refers to this type of woman as a silly woman. Are you a silly woman? Well, you may have been a silly woman all year, but are you ready to stop the madness, now? Stop playing house. A real man of God will ask for your hand in marriage in due season and marry you. He will not just keep stringing you along.

Don't make large investments in this man if he is not going to settle down with you and especially if he's not right. Be honest with yourself. This is one of the most important decisions in your life. It will affect your mind, soul, and body in the long run if you continue to let yourself be abused. KNOW THAT YOU ARE VALUABLE AND NOT BECAUSE OF WHAT YOU CAN GIVE AWAY!

YOU CAN'T FORCE SOMEONE TO CHANGE

As you probably have already discovered, love can be very one-sided. If your so-called significant other doesn't really pay any real attention to you, he is more than likely trying to find a way out of the relationship. If you stop for a moment and are honest with yourself and you realize that you have been trying to *make* this man or woman be with you and care about you, there is just one thing that you need to realize right now.

You cannot force someone to love you! God himself gives us a free will.

Who wants someone that is forced to love them? Forced love could never be real love! Who could get any real satisfaction out of something not real? Anyone who can get satisfaction out of making someone love them is obviously not too well in the head and is probably some kind of serial killer. Think about it.

ALWAYS PUT YOURSELF IN SOMEONE ELSE'S SHOES

If you're thinking of cheating on your wife, think about the times when you make love to her and how the two of you enjoy your time together. And, while you're enjoying each other, you suddenly say to her, "I love you." By doing this, you have created an even greater emotional tie with her.

Now, what I want you to do is imagine something for me. Imagine her being sexually active with someone else *in the same feeling, cheating on you.*

Doesn't feel too good does it?

NEVER LET SOMEONE DISRESPECT YOU

Be encouraging and compassionate toward others.

If being rude means not putting up with other people's nonsense, so be it.

The first sign of disrespect is when he is disrespectful to you. It is one thing to submit to your husband or some authority in righteousness, but it is an entirely different thing to be treated like crap subjecting yourself to emotional, mental, and physical abuse.

WAKE UP! Do not go into denial.

DROP HIM OR HER!

Let me ask you this question, why are you dealing with a disrespectful person? Do you enjoy being disrespected? Do you enjoy being talked down to or lied to?

Most people that are disrespectful are pride-filled people. Oh, but not on King's Watch! I'm here to help you to wake up! You *will* wake up, change your mindset, and feel more confident to move on. Just read on.

These types of people rarely change because, for one, they, generally, like being the way that they are, and if they are not seeking to humble or better themselves, then you certainly cannot teach them by staying in a sad, unproductive relationship. They only see you as a naïve, easy to manipulate individual.

BE A MENTOR (HELP OTHERS IN NEED)

Be a mentor. Use the very experiences that you have been through to help open up other people's eyes.

Support those going through depression. Once you become enlightened, you can now reach out to others.

The world would be a better place if we would assist in uplifting others, in being loyal, and respectful to one another.

NOT EVERY PERSON LOVES THE SAME

Women are emotional creatures and men desire to be respected.

People never pay attention to how they are loving the other person, whether they are treating them kindly or not? They just assume that everything and everyone in their lives are okay.

So you loved hard and invested your heart into a dead beat.

Well, let it stop here!

Loving someone that doesn't call, text, or check on you is outright foolish! Ain't nobody got time for that! It is truly time for you to realize that you are not a second-hand store that he or she can just walk in and out of whenever he or she pleases!

NOT EVERY SITUATION CALLS FOR A REACTION

Don't let him see you sweat! BE COOL AND CALM! If he sees you sweat, his head gets pumped up.

Somebody will come along and love you the way you ought to be loved.

Just breathe and keep on living.

My desire is that every woman in the world has a stable and healthy mindset to know that God has designed a specific man just for her as well as designed her specifically for a certain man to raise children or to be in a relationship with to accomplish the perfect will of God for their lives.

In the Book of Corinthians the seventh chapter, God said, "Let every man have his *own* wife!" So, you just need to wait on the Lord and trust in Him. In due season, according to God's will for your life, it will happen.

You must understand that you have to be at peace and have a strong mind to wait. There's so much more to life than just being in a relationship with a man or a woman to make you feel worthy. You are a worthy individual whether you have a man or woman in your life or not. There's so much more to occupy your time. Discover those things. The world is filled with plenty good and wonderful things to keep you engaged.

OPEN YOUR EYES BEFORE IT IS TOO LATE—It only takes one day

One day, you just might catch a disease from him or her.

One day, you just might die because of all of the abuse and violence around you.

Yes, one day, you just might lose all of the time and energy that you put in.

And, this will not just affect you but all others that are connected to you.

Be honest and straightforward!
Do not be a manipulator!
Stop playing games!

One day you might sincerely fall in love, but you will be reminded of all of the things that you did to others.

This hurts.

Listen please!

Just leave when you have the opportunity.

YOU DESERVE BETTER

You deserve better!

You deserve some peace and satisfaction, don't you?

Now, you know that you have not been satisfied in a long time. Not being happy can really be a weight in a relationship. Does it make sense to just exist in a relationship that you sincerely know is not of God? I'm not talking to married folks that are just going through a dry time but they know that they were meant to be. I'm talking to people who know that they're in a crazy, controlling, manipulating relationship and know in their hearts that they just simply need to RUN!

You deserve someone that wants you to succeed!

BEING ALONE

Today, you're feeling down thinking about how silly you were to allow this man or woman to go as far as you did.

You feel humiliated.

But, it's not your loss. It's their loss.

Their value is far less than yours. Their outlook is far worse than yours.
You, now, believe in yourself and know, now, that God has a really great plan for your life because you finally woke up.

Just think about how it would be if you were still in that messy relationship allowing yourself to be used and abused. Thank God for the removal of all of that garbage and excess baggage.

I know that you hate being alone, but guess what? You were, already, alone in the relationship. Yes!

Now, you can be in a room and finally get noticed by someone who will truly love you.

I am so happy you are okay.

NEVER GIVE MORE ATTENTION THAN YOU RECEIVE

Have you ever felt like the very person that you want is really not feeling you?

You're feeling like it's your fault because he or she is flipping the script on you.

And, you keep taking the blame because you feel you love them, but that's not love. That's a soul tie that needs to be broken!

You did nothing wrong and let's keep it that way.

Don't let anyone change your beautiful heart.

I feel that you want revenge.

Well if you want revenge, your revenge is to keep living and to stay happy. That's the best revenge you can have. That's a killer one.

SUICIDE IS NOT AN OPTION

When you are not experiencing happiness in your relationship anymore, this is a sign that you need to do some self-re-evaluation and research how you could either better the relationship or get out of the relationship before it is too late.

My heart is hurting as I write this book BECAUSE I WANT THE BEST FOR YOU!

It is hurting because I was once that man that you are trying so hard to break soul ties from. But now I am excited about how I've had a change of heart for the better. It is my goal to treat females with the respect they deserve.

Since I was definitely one of those men I'm writing about, my advice to you is to focus on yourself and your children if you have any instead of brooding over someone who doesn't care whether you live or die.

You must know that the person that you would commit suicide over will continue to date and live on.

So commit yourself to increasing your self-esteem not to committing suicide!

Sad events in life get better with time and change will happen in your life whether you want it to or not. It is a matter of how much change you want and what level of change you desire.

If someone calls you a negative name then you must be strong enough to reject that in your mental and spiritual ear.

Get ready to prepare yourself to live!

Focus on what you can do to better yourself.

WORK, ATTEND CHURCH, READ POSITIVE BOOKS, AND STAY AROUND GREATER MINDED PEOPLE.

If he or she is not ready for a relationship, it is for a good reason. Don't try to force someone to be with you. It won't be real love!

DON'T MISPLACE YOUR TRUST

The Bible teaches us to trust in the Lord with *all* of our hearts and to lean not to our own understanding (Proverbs 3:5-6).

When we place *all* of our trust in man, this is when we make a huge mistake and end up hurt, every time.

Jumping to the wrong conclusions will always start an argument and a misunderstanding in any relationship. No one likes to be accused of something that's not correct.

Know the facts before you accuse a person.

People start accusing, oftentimes, when they are in fear of losing someone or something.

My grandmother often said to me, "If a person is always accusing you of something that is not true, more than likely the person making the accusations is the *guilty* party in some kind of way or is suffering from some sort of low self-esteem or walking in fear of losing someone or something."

The accuser may, also, more than likely be the one who is messing around! So Beware!

LIFE GOES ON

Will you get over it? Yes you will!

Time heals all wounds. It may not seem like it, right now, but time will heal you.

Baby girl, can you do Mr. King a favor, LOVE YOURSELF MORE!

I need you to take care of yourself.
Go out and get your nails and your hair done!

When you sit up and worry about someone who is not treating you right, you more than likely are not even eating.

STOP WORRYING. Make up your mind to stop this madness! Direct your thoughts in the right direction. Think on good and positive things! Take care of yourself!

Take some time out for yourself. Go and have dinner at a really nice restaurant. Pamper yourself a little. Have a good time.

In due season, God will bring your king into your life to pamper you and love you, correctly.

Laugh and be happy!

This is good for your soul.

COMPATIBILITY IS KEY

Don't allow yourself to be tolerated. Go where you are celebrated!

It's vital to be with someone who thinks like you, wants to grow with you, is proud to have you, and is happy to commit to you.

If you cook, clean, and have sexual relations with someone who is not your soul mate, you are wasting your valuable time as well as his or hers. You need to be nourished properly in every capacity of your being including your mind and emotions, and when you are with the wrong mate, you are unfulfilled in just about every way! Your mind becomes troubled and burdened, and your emotions become dejected and gloomy.

It is truly worth it to be patient and to wait for your compatible mate.

HEALING TAKES TIME

Allow your mind and soul time to heal.
Stop contacting him or her.
Just stop the madness!

You say, "I just want to hear his voice or her voice?" Really?

Do you enjoy being hurt? So, you like taking part in helping someone to disgrace you?

Each and every time you call, you expect him or her to say something that you want to hear, right, but the exact opposite happens!

Stop it! Just stop it! Does it make any sense to stay with someone who keeps bringing you pain?

You won't heal if you do.

No texts, no calls, no wandering over to the house to catch him or her in anything to prove you were right. It won't stop anything. He or she will just continue to do their thing!

Just stop the madness!

Please listen and pay close attention! You must follow instructions to be healed!

GOD IS THE ONLY MAN YOU NEED AT THIS TIME

During your time of healing, Jesus is the only Man that you will need during this time! Why? Because you've been so hurt in that relationship that you're in no condition, neither spiritually, emotionally, mentally, or physically to be in a new relationship, right now. You would destroy the relationship, yourself, at this point because of your trust issues and emotional issues that need to be settled.

My advice to you is to use this stage in your life to spend quality time getting to know your creator – the one who knows all about marriage, real love, and healthy relationships. You'll need this time with Him to get healed, to be restored, and to gain the knowledge that you'll need to be fruitful and productive in the right and true relationship when it comes along.

God will send you the right soul mate at the right appointed time, and then you will have to trust again. Putting trust in a man is a hard thing to do after you've been hurt by man.

But because you will have taken out quality time to spend with God, He will give you what you need to trust again and to make wise decisions.

ENOUGH IS ENOUGH (I'M DONE)

He lies to you over and over again – no, not just once or twice. He is an impulsive liar.

He doesn't care if you know it, either. He doesn't care if you know about anything he does.

He will not be the one to close this door that he knows need to be closed nor will he tell you that he really doesn't want you. Oh, no, not as long as he can keep you hanging around like a spare tire and use and abuse you.

That's right. He doesn't want you, but he doesn't want anyone else to have you, either even though he may have several other relationships going on the side.

Understand something. Don't get it twisted. Just because he doesn't want anyone else to have you, does not mean that he wants you. If he really did, he would treat you better and commit to you only, my dear.

Enough is enough!

I know that you see this and now it's time for you to wake up!

LETTING GO OF NEGATIVE PEOPLE AND NEGATIVITY

One of the hardest things you will ever have to do is to stop being naïve and to make up your mind to get out of denial.

I say that you're in denial because you fell for this person and you are emotionally tied to this person, yet he or she does not have any real emotional tie to you and, yet, you refuse to admit this to yourself.

Love should not be this hard.

The more you wake up, this walk and journey gets easier to just LET GO!

DON'T DISRESPECT YOURSELF

Stay faithful to your task. Stay on point and focused.

Never let haters disrespect you, your dreams, or your vision.

You forgot your vision and dreams because of this man or woman.

But, now, it's time to respect yourself enough to get back on task.

A REAL MAN SEES ONLY YOU

There is a movie called "When a Man Loves a Woman" starring Meg Ryan. In the movie, Meg Ryan becomes an alcoholic. As a result, her marriage and children were just about destroyed. But it was the *mutual* true love that they had for *one another* that brought them back together, and her husband's stance that said, "I know who and what she was before this." So, he stood by her and watched her become whole again even though it was really hard.

During the time of their separation, her husband did not get involved with anyone else even through their hardest moments. *He only had eyes for her* even when she was at her lowest, but pressing in to get better.

VENTING IS GOOD

Do not vent to everybody, but when you have a need to vent, vent to someone that you truly believe you can trust with your information.

However, the best way to vent is to fall on your knees, often, and pray to the One who has all of the answers!

You will feel a whole lot better!

BEING SINGLE IS BETTER THAN BEING PLAYED

I would rather be single any day than to put up with a counterfeit relationship.

It is EASIER TO THINK AND PLAN for your future when you are ALONE without distractions.

So embrace your singleness and wait until your appointed time.

The Bible teaches us to be anxious for nothing (Philippians 4:6-8).

LISTEN TO HER

There was a time when society believed in a man being a gentleman and in a woman conducting herself, respectfully, as a lady.

If your mate is trying to communicate to you how she feels, listen to her.

Now, listening is not just saying yes after every sentence that she says or repeating what she just said.

Listening is responding to her request accordingly because you have listened effectively.

When you really listen well, you will give a proper response.

The Bible teaches us not to be just hearers of the word, but doers of the word (James 1:22).

You will wish you would have listened to her after she has left you and, now, you hear that someone else is listening to her.

IT'S THEIR LOSS

When you lose someone you've spent so much time investing in, it feels like a loss. But the real prize was you, queen.

It is the other person's loss – the one who gave no respect.

Unfortunately, the next person who enters into a relationship with him or her will get all of that negativity, disrespect, and nonsense that you left behind.

Who would miss that?

SEPARATION CAN BE A GOOD THING

When God chooses to separate people, it is for a reason. God will even allow things to occur in our lives to block people from affecting our lives in a negative way.

If or when he does bring people back together, it is, always, for a greater purpose. It's often because there will now be a more mature association.

The fact that we will not always live forever and will be separated from even our loved ones one day should help us to make better decisions while we are alive. Many people live to be at least in their 70s or 80s, but not a whole lot of people live past this age. However, tomorrow is not promised to any of us. So, age really doesn't even matter does it? We all know about young people who have died and left this earth.

Some people, who made me the happiest in my life, have already separated from this life and crossed over.

People are only loaned to us for a while. We are all God's creation. So, we all have to answer to Him in the end.

So, stop acting like you can't do without a man or a woman who could care less about you. If he or she died today or tomorrow, what are you going to do? Jump in the casket, too?

Many of us have lost loved ones and those people at least cared about us! My grandfather was someone I lost a couple of years ago, and God gave us the strength to live on because if you trust in Him for strength, He will give it to you. You will see that family member or friend that you loved so much again someday because you both trusted in the Savior.

So, understand this once and for all. No man is our God. No woman is our God. God is our God. Seek Him first and keep Him first.

When we place things in its proper order and *seek God first* and *keep Him first*, He will give us the right mate in due season.

LET'S TALK (COMMUNICATION IS EVERYTHING)

Leaving things unsaid or walking away from confrontation is not always good.

Talk it out, but do not argue when God gives you a second chance at love and TRUST.

JUST LISTEN!

REAL MEN TAKE CARE OF THEIR KIDS

A *real* man takes care of his children without anyone telling him to do so.

A lot of you little boys and girls are allowing your new partner to keep you away from your children and allowing him or her to dictate this to you.

How can you not be compassionate toward your children? They are a part of your being! There are numerous families in this world who have ready-made families. You can respect your new spouse and still maintain a good relationship with your children. You need to stand for what is right which also includes making sure that your children also respect your new spouse.

You are also responsible for respecting your ex's new spouse as well. Your children need a good father and a good, moral role model in their lives.

PAY ATTENTION TO THESE SIGNS!

If you can go a whole day without talking to me, then I know where we stand.

You obviously consider me to be a part-time lover or friend.

NEVER BEG FOR ATTENTION

You should never have to force a person to do anything or force them to be in your life.

There was a song in the 70s called, "If it Don't fit, Don't Force it, Just Relax and Let it Go!"

This is true. So many times, people try to make people fit into their lives when they know it's not a match or a good fit at all. They don't even care if the person is married or not – just begging for attention. Anyone will just about do.

If this person cannot bring you into a greater and more peaceful lifestyle, he or she will do nothing more for you than be a kink in your chain.

GOING YOUR OWN WAY

You visualize your significant other making you smile, but instead he or she does nothing but hurt you over and over again. Yes, he pushes you away to the point of finally making the wise decision to go your own way - SO BE IT!

A wake-up call is always good. At a hotel stay, the front desk clerk calls you at a certain time so that you will not over sleep.

When your significant other continuously hurts you, it is also a wake-up call for you not to stay asleep too long in that bad relationship. I can feel your thoughts. You want to go your own way - SO BE IT! GO!

There are things that you WANT TO ACCOMPLISH and this person is keeping you around just to prevent you from moving forward and to treat you badly.

Take a stand!

LEARN FROM YOUR RELATIONSHIP

If you're ignored in your relationship as if you are not important, it is time for you to learn from this situation and give him or her some space.

It is good to space yourself from someone who ignores you, anyway. Don't you think?

RELATIONSHIP GOALS

Make sure that you and your mate have compatible goals. Do you both have goals in your life? Does each of your goals fit into each other's lives? It is vital that you both are on one accord in every area of your life, otherwise there will be very little agreement in your life and you are destined to either depart from each other or to just exist in the relationship.

Your belief system should be very much the same including spiritual beliefs, familial beliefs (courting, religion, sex before marriage, marriage concepts, children, how to raise a family, etc.), as well as monetary and business handling and so much more.

It is so important for couples to be equally yoked. That is, to have someone whom you have so much in common with and you believe the same things. You are like-minded. Two people can't continue on the same path if they are not in agreement.

Once you have been linked together with the right person, be sure to listen to each other and be compassionate toward each other. Communication and balance is key. You are in this together.

BE HUMBLE

I have grown so much! Yet, we are all lifelong learners. Always keep your heart open to learn and to become strengthened to make wiser decisions.

DON'T LET IDIOTS DRAIN YOUR DAY

Never allow people to come into your atmosphere and ruin your day.

You have too much to accomplish and you don't want to waste any of your time.

Don't ponder on someone else's garbage too long. If you do, it will start to stink.

Stinking thinking affects your ability to think effectively or to work and get things done.

RESPECT WOMEN

Men who are not mature are nothing more than little boys. They laugh at putting women through a living hell.

They make mockery of how she cries for him, and then tell their friends all about it and how naïve she is. Men don't take the time to realize that they, too, will have daughters one day and some man could very well treat their daughters in the same disrespectful way.

This is not a joke. Love and respect your woman in the same way that you would want your daughters to be treated. Your mother is a woman, too. Would you want someone to disrespect your mother and treat her badly?

SOMETIMES YOU HAVE TO GET HURT
TO WAKE UP

Pain hurts but if you never have pain, you will never know where you need healing nor will you be able to get the proper diagnosis.

Deep hurt is the worst kind. But, you can either allow it to destroy you or you can allow it to cause you to realize that you are a human being with feelings, and then rise up in righteous indignation and kick old boy or old girl to the curve!

Get back to your true self.

GOOD THINGS COME TO THOSE WHO WAIT

Think about this. When you give your body to a little boy he tells his buddies all about it.

A REAL MAN WILL ASK FOR YOUR HAND IN MARRIAGE not just your body.

A real man knows how to wait and not rush sex.

If he is rushing you it is for a reason. He wants to brag to his buddies about how easy it was to manipulate you or he wants to quickly have sex with you and just get rid of you.

Think of yourself as a discerning woman who desires to be treated like a queen by the right man. A queen knows that good things come to those who wait.

Who wants a jealous, overprotective, annoying woman? Absolutely no one.

However, she may be jealous for a reason.

Some women are jealous simply because that's their nature and they, simply, refuse to submit themselves to changing for the better. She enjoys being overpowering and controlling and acting like she's crazy. This type of woman, a good man should run from.

But, some women are jealous because they've been hurt in the past and never received the healing that they so desperately needed from insecurity and low self-esteem in order to be whole and to be capable of trusting again.

However, there are some women who are jealous because they are simply not getting enough attention from their mates.

Men, you can help your mate to be even more secure in the relationship when you treat your one and only like the queen she is to you. And, women, you will have the responsibility to *return* the respect and honor when you have that right mate in your life.

Now get this...some women are in relationships and settle for believing that they're the main 'whore.' There is no such thing. He is playing you big time. He really doesn't care for *any* of you – not whore #1, 2 or 3. If he did, he'd commit to *one* of you!

And, women…never be foolish enough to consider yourself to be the main 'whore' in a relationship with a man. Respect yourself more than that!

THE PROVERBS 31 WOMEN ARE THE BEST ONES

She is definitely worth it. She is a teacher, a mentor - a Proverbs 31 woman.

God fashioned her. She even thinks on both sides of her brain.

She is not intimidating, prideful, vain, or arrogant. Though she is a strong and confident woman. She is made to think and reason well, yes, the Proverbs 31 woman, and with this gift – she is your helpmeet.

Love her and appreciate her. She is definitely worth it! Surely, I'm talking about you, queen.

But, if you haven't already ascertained to become this praiseworthy woman, then take some time out to study her and become her.

When your mean and evil ex tries to come back into your life to see if you are happy, do not let your guard down.

Tell him, "I do not give second chances and I am busy being productive now."

Say only what you need to say and DO NOT prolong the conversation. Do not go to places where you know he or she will be. Keep your distance. Stay out of strife.

Be like Tina Turner with Ike. She made up her mind to never go back to Ike. Instead, she went back to her true self.

NEVER GO HARD FOR SOMEONE WHO DOESN'T GO HARD FOR YOU

You will get exhausted trying to make the wrong people happy. Stop entertaining the wrong woman or man.

Late night sex booty calls, and calls to clean his house, to cook, pay his or her rent, or give up all your money has grown very tired. Don't you think?

Just stop the madness! You are being used to the max and investing time and energy in the wrong somebody!

Can I get an AMEN?

TOUGHEN UP

You can be a good person at heart but if you are tolerating being treated with contempt, you need to toughen up.

I am going to provide you with some good advice to toughen you up.

1. Feed your mind with positive words.
2. Recognize who you are.
3. Discover your purpose.
4. Know that God made you for *His* GLORY.
5. Exercising Discipline and Patience will help you not to get involved in situations too quickly. It will also help you to make better decisions in life. These are also attributes of God, your creator.

These are just a few suggestions that you can follow to make you stronger.

LOVE AND RESPECT YOUR PARENTS

If you see the person that you're interested in disrespecting his or her parents, this is a great warning sign that he or she will also disrespect.

Shout out to my parents for creating and teaching me how to respect women.

My mom is a pastor and an advocate for women and I miss my dad so much.

I love them so much and I strongly believe that this is one of the reasons why I have become a mentor to many people. I have also become very compassionate about how women are to be treated. Once again, this is because I was one of those guys that women need to run from.

BUT I'VE LEARNED SO MUCH OVER THE YEARS BECAUSE I MADE A CHOICE TO FINALLY *LISTEN* AND I'M STILL LEARNING! NEVER STOP LEARNING!

SO JUST LISTEN!

YOU TOO CAN HAVE A GOOD MAN

Yes, you can have a good man. You only need to be willing and patient to wait on your appointed time.

Women who sincerely trust in God are part of the royal generation that God has established. And, if you are trusting in God for your mate, you must realize that according to His perfect will, He has designed a person just for you who knows exactly how to treat you.

This chosen person for you will willingly want to learn what pleases you and what does not please you and you will have the same opportunity to be a blessing to him in return resulting in a wonderful union.

NEVER CHEAT

Don't cheat yourself out of happiness.

To cheat when another person cheats just to get back at him or her is cheating yourself out of your real assignment and it causes you to lower your own standards.

WHAT IS MEANT TO BE WILL COME TO PASS

Stop forcing yourself to be with someone whom you cannot change.

You are not the one who is supposed to change the person anyway. God changes a man or woman as he or she submits to Him.

Your good decisions will create an environment for change in your *own* life. Always.

STOP ENTERTAINING A FALSE RELATIONSHIP

Stop hitting people up. In other words, stop calling and obsessing.

If the person is sincerely interested in you, he or she will miss you and call *you*. But if the person does not check on you, *frequently and consistently*, then he or she is simply not interested.

Stop being the one to always call, text, or the one who pays more attention.

This should be an equally yoked relationship – one that is of the same spirit and mindset – yes, on the same page!

IF IT IS MEANT TO BE, TRUST ME, YOU WILL MEET AGAIN AT THE RIGHT TIME. IF HE IS NOT THE RIGHT ONE, YOUR TRULY DESIGNED MATE WILL COME INSTEAD. SO GET PREPARED BY LEARNING MORE!

LISTEN AND DO NOT WALK AWAY

YOU YOUNG GUYS NEED TO GROW UP AND BE A MAN.

LOVE YOUR WOMAN RIGHT AND DISCIPLINE YOURSELF. She needs you to listen to her. Sometimes, she feels lonely and she needs your input on something or just desires to spend time with you.

Some men and women take it too far, however, thinking that a man or woman can fill an empty void in their lives or they believe that a man or woman will meet all of their needs. Not so. This is why you're empty. Baby girl, young man - when you are lonely look to God. Your help comes from the Lord!

He is the only one who can *rightly* fill a void in your life. He is the only one who can supply *all* of your needs, not a man or a woman.

God never intended for the mate He gives us to take His place. Keep that in mind. God will have to remain first in your life even when you get your mate!

RECOGNIZE THE GAME

Guys will fill your head with sweet nothings and lies. A lot of guys are charming.

This is how they get you with their charm! They are very appealing and will shower you with all kinds of compliments, luring you in with their pretty smile and charming words. Yes, whispering sweet nothings in your ears. So, you've got to recognize the game, ladies.

Women love attention and romance! But, if it's nothing but game, how does the attention and romance benefit you?

Guys will even cry and do just about anything when running game on you.

Open your eyes and ears, women, and end the game.

END THE GAME

Yes, it's true. It's usually men who are the ones running game, but women if you don't want game run on you, then you will need to make some revisions yourself!

Too many of you use your bodies to seduce men. You're half naked and you dress like a thot. Your purpose is for every man that you come in contact with to gawk at you. If your body were only for your husband, your one and only man, you'd dress like that *only* for him in private!

You charm men with your soft, seductive voices to manipulate and lure him into your cunning traps, not realizing at all that there's only one type of man interested in a woman who dresses and acts like that.

And, so, now that you've got him, the script has flipped on you, you say. You didn't know you were alluring a dog with his tongue hanging out to the side. And, now you're shocked that he's doing nothing but running game on you?

No real, mature, and disciplined man with a clear head on his shoulders wants a woman who dresses and acts like a whore. So, guess what, when you dress overly sexy and act like that, that's how he sees you – as a woman who is out to attract nothing but sex. So, that's what he wants from you - to just have sex with you. Really! Not to establish a real and meaningful relationship with you.

There's no commitment on his part. Sex is only on his mind. And you're shocked? Why? Didn't you lure him in with your body and flimsy clothing showing off your goodies?

Then you shouldn't be shocked at all. Of course, that's all he wants.

And, because you're a woman and more emotional in nature, you're all caught up, now.

IT'S TIME TO CHANGE THE GAME, LADIES. IF YOU WANT A REAL MAN, YOU'VE GOT TO BECOME A REAL WOMAN.

Remember the **Proverbs 31 woman**. If you haven't already ascertained to become this praiseworthy woman, then take some time out to study her and become her.

A LOYAL MAN IS A GREAT MAN

For some reason, men have always thought that having sex with many females is what makes them a man.

But, a man who can commit to one woman and treat her right is what makes a man – and a great man, at that.

A disciplined man who commits his heart to one woman is a gentleman that will receive honor.

Woman, *stop* giving your GIFT AWAY FOR NOTHING!

You are special and God gave you a gift that must be taken care of. It is fragile and must be handled with care by your husband and only your husband.

LAST WORDS

I hope that you, now, have all of the necessary tools to take you to the next level of learning to keep you steadfast and unmovable always abounding in the work of the Lord Jesus.

You are remarkably beautiful and I am elated about your new season.

77089537R00055

Made in the USA
Lexington, KY
22 December 2017